WHAT IS THE GI?

CATHERINE PROCTOR

Jane Curry Publishing

Catherine Proctor is a freelance writer and editor who specialises in health and cookery books. She runs her own cookery school and lives on Sydney's Northern Beaches with her husband and two children.

Her other books include: *High Flavour Low Fat* and *How Much Carb? How Much Protein?*

First published by Jane Curry Publishing
(Wentworth Concepts T/A) 2005
PO Box 780, Edgecliff, NSW 2027
www.janecurrypublishing.com.au

Reprinted 2005 and 2011

All rights reserved. No part of this book may be reproduced or transmitted in any form or by any means, electronic or mechanical, including photocopying, recording or by any other information storage or retrieval system, without prior permission in writing from the publisher.

National Library of Australia
Cataloguing-in-publication data:

Proctor, Catherine.
What's the GI? lose weight and stay healthy using the glycemic index.

ISBN 978-1-920727-16-1.

1. Glycemic index. 2. Food - Carbohydrate content. 3. Reducing diets. I. Title.
613.25

Cover and internal design: Deborah Parry Graphics
Typeset in Carniola 12/15pt
Printed in China by Everbest Printing Company Ltd.

CONTENTS

Introduction		5
1	What is the GI?	7
2	What is a GI diet?	13
3	Ten reasons to eat low GI foods	15
4	Carbohydrates	20
5	Fruit and vegetables	25
6	Drinks	28
7	Fats and proteins	29
8	GI for the family	32
9	Easy ways to lower your GI	34
10	Eating out and take away foods	36
11	GI counter - food categories	40
12	GI counter - alphabetical listings	58

INTRODUCTION

GI is an abbreviation of the glycemic index. The glycemic index is a way of measuring how quickly carbohydrates affect our blood sugar levels.

Foods that have a high GI break down quickly and have a fairly immediate impact on our blood sugar levels. Foods that have a low GI are digested more slowly by our bodies. These foods keep our blood sugar levels more stable. If there is no carbohydrate in a food, there is no GI rating.

The GI is not intended to be used as the sole determiner of how to eat. Many low GI foods contain high levels of fat and or sodium, which is why it is important to use the GI rating of a food within the context of the basic principles of healthy eating, that is eating a balanced diet including all the food groups and exercising regularly.

This handy pocket guide will give you all the information you need to turn your diet around and get you on the path to losing weight, having greater sustained energy levels and better health.

CHAPTER 1
WHAT IS THE GI?

Our bodies have three main sources of energy: carbohydrates, protein and fats. Carbohydrates are basically sugars and starches. Examples of carbohydrates include:

- Sugar
- Flour
- Potatoes
- Pasta
- Bread
- Rice
- Grains and pulses
- Fruit
- Vegetables

How do carbohydrates affect our blood sugar levels?

When we eat carbohydrates they are quickly absorbed by our bodies and they affect our blood sugar levels. When our blood sugar levels rise a hormone called insulin is released into our bloodstream to regulate our blood sugar levels. When our blood sugar levels rise rapidly insulin counters the effect of the carbohydrate by causing the blood sugar level to fall.

When our blood sugar levels drop we feel tired and listless and we crave more carbohydrates. If we then eat more carbs, more insulin is released and the cycle continues.

What is the GI?

GI is an abbreviation of the glycemic index. The glycemic index is a way of measuring how quickly carbohydrates affect our blood sugar levels.

Foods that have a high GI (70+) are those that break down quickly and have a fairly immediate impact on our blood sugar levels, such as sliced white bread and potatoes.

Medium GI foods (with a rating of 50-70) have a moderately fast impact on blood sugar levels. Examples include Weet-Bix, dried fruit and ice-cream.

Foods that have a low GI (-50), such as oats, whole grains, and low-fat yogurt, are those that are digested more slowly by our bodies. These foods keep our blood sugar levels more stable.

What makes some foods lower in GI than others?

There are two factors that affect the GI of all foods:

The type of food. Pure proteins and fats contain no carbohydrate and as a result they do not affect blood sugar levels. They have a GI rating of 0. The glycemic index is a measure of how quickly carbohydrates affect our blood sugar levels—it does not measure proteins and fats.

The speed at which a food is digested. The longer a food takes to digest, the lower the GI.

The speed at which a food is digested depends upon:

The amount of fibre. Fibre slows down the time that it takes your body to digest a food. Therefore foods that are high in fibre have a lower GI than those that contain little or no fibre.

The type of sugar. Glucose raises blood sugar rapidly, sucrose (white sugar) has a medium GI, while both fructose (fruit sugar) and lactose (dairy sugar) converts slowly.

The amount of fat. Because fat slows down the rate at which food leaves the stomach, high fat foods slow the rate at which blood sugar levels rise. Therefore high fat foods have a lower GI.

How processed the food is. Raw foods and those with large particles (such as whole grains rather than grains that have been milled) take the body longer to digest and therefore cause blood sugar levels to rise more slowly. Foods that are highly refined and processed (such as white bread) are digested immediately and have a high GI.

The amount of acid. Foods with a high level of acid (such as citrus and vinegar) move more slowly through the digestive system.

Understanding the GI

The GI is not intended to be used as the sole determiner of how to eat. The basic principles of healthy eating remain:

Eat more fruit and vegetables. These are full of vitamins, minerals and fibre. Try to eat between five and seven servings a day.

Eat more whole grains and cereals. Fibre is essential for intestinal health, it fills you up for longer because it is slower to digest and reduces the GI levels of foods.

Drink more water. Try to drink at least two litres of water a day to maintain optimal health. Water is GI-free, carb-free, and fat-free. It keeps you hydrated, is essential to your body's needs and it will fill you up.

Use the right fats. Olive oil is far better for your heart and overall health than butter or margarine. Healthy fats are the monounsaturated fats found in vegetables (olives, nuts, seeds, avocadoes, as well as the oils made from these) and the polyunsaturated fats that come from oily fish, such as trout and salmon. Avoid the saturated fats (such as butter, meat fat, full-fat dairy products) and transfats (palm oil, margarine, commercial cakes and biscuits) as these have serious health risks (see Chapter 6).

Eat more nuts and pulses. These are cheap and filling and highly nutritious.

Eat more seafood and less red meat. The fats in seafood are far better for overall health than the saturated fats found in red meat. Lean red meat is a good option but you still should aim for at least 3 serves of fish a week to benefit from the polyunsaturated fats that are found in seafood.

Not all high GI foods should be avoided

To understand the GI properly you need to assess the amount of carbohydrate in a food. Watermelon is a good example of this. It has a high GI because its sweetness comes from glucose rather than the fructose that most fruits contain (and glucose has a much higher GI than fructose). Although its GI is high, its impact on blood sugar levels is far less than that of other high GI foods because it actually contains very little carbohydrate.

Not all low GI foods are healthy

If you used the GI in isolation to choose what types of food to eat you would find yourself eating many foods high in fat (because they have a very low GI), and avoiding some essential vegetables and fruits (because they have a high GI). Many low GI foods contain high levels of fat and or sodium, which is why it is important to use the GI rating of a food within the context of the basic principles of healthy eating.

CHAPTER 2
WHAT IS A GI DIET?

Using the GI — a new way of thinking about food

With a GI diet you understand how food is absorbed by your body and what effect different foods have on your metabolism. Once you understand how your digestive system works it is easier to make the right food choices and to take responsibility for your diet.

This is not a fad

GI diets are based on medical research and a scientific understanding of how our bodies work. The principles that underlie GI diets have been used to help control diabetes for many years.

No food groups are eliminated
With every food group there are low GI choices that will satisfy your cravings and help you lose weight at the same time. The GI Diet does not ban all carbs—instead it outlines what are the right sort of carbs to help you lose weight.

It is filling — you will never be hungry
Low GI foods provide a slow release of energy and are high in fibre which fills you up.

There are many health benefits apart from weight loss
These include decreased risk of heart attack and stroke, better skin condition, fewer mood swings, more energy, control of blood sugar levels, a reduction in cravings between meals, and the control and prevention of diabetes.

It is sustainable over a long period of time
Because a GI diet is about balanced, healthy eating it is not like other diets that eliminate certain food groups. It can be used as a blueprint for a healthy, sustainable new way of thinking about eating.

CHAPTER 3
TEN REASONS TO EAT LOW GI FOODS

Scientific research has proved that there are many health benefits from eating low GI foods. These include:

1. Weight loss
2. Decreased chance of stroke and heart attack
3. A reduction in cravings between meals
4. Increase in energy levels
5. Elimination of mood swings
6. Improved skin condition
7. Control and prevention of diabetes
8. Reduction in weight gain during pregnancy
9. Boost your body's immune system
10. Overall improvement in health

1. Weight loss

There are two ways in which low GI foods help you lose weight. Firstly, because they are higher in fibre and more slowly absorbed into your digestive system, low GI foods keep you feeling full for longer. This reduces the amount of food you will consume.

When you eat high GI foods the insulin in your body has to immediately deal with the excess blood sugar in order to regulate your blood sugar levels. It does this by storing the excess sugars as fat. So by eating low GI foods you are also preventing the storage of excess sugars as fat.

2. Decreased chance of stroke and heart attack

When blood glucose levels are kept steady it helps prevent atherosclerosis (hardening of the arteries), as well as the formation of blood clots.

3. A reduction in cravings between meals

Cravings occur when blood sugar levels drop. High GI foods cause blood sugar levels to rapidly rise and then fall, causing cravings between meals.

Low GI food reduce these cravings by preventing excessive swings in blood sugar levels.

4. Increase in energy levels
Low GI foods will help raise your energy levels for the same reason that they help reduce cravings: the prevention of rapid swings in blood sugar levels. Low GI foods give a slow sustained release of energy.

5. Elimination of mood swings
One of the reasons why we crave carbs is because they stimulate production of serotonin, a hormone that makes us feel good. High GI foods create a quick mood boost, but this is quickly followed by a mood slump. Low GI foods will give a gradual release of serotonin, helping prevent mood swings.

6. Improved skin condition
High insulin levels (which are the body's natural response to high GI foods) trigger excess sebum production. This in turn can lead to oily skin, blocked pores and acne.

7. Control and prevention of diabetes
If you already suffer from diabetes, switching to a low GI diet can help you control your blood sugar levels and control the effects of diabetes. A low GI diet can also prevent type 2 (adult onset) diabetes from developing.

8. Reduction in weight gain during pregnancy
Studies now suggest that eating a low GI diet helps keep the kilos off during pregnancy. Mothers eating a high GI diet also have heavier babies with a higher body fat.

9. Boost your body's immune system
Foods high in sugar prevent white blood cells from functioning at their maximum capacity when trying to fight illness. A low GI diet allows white cells to do their job, thereby helping to prevent illnesses such as colds and flu.

10. Overall improvement in health
Low GI foods are less processed, higher in fibre and full of vitamins and minerals. They provide a

slow steady release of energy and keep you feeling calm and sustained. As well as the health benefits listed above, low GI foods are linked to higher IQs, longer life expectancy, a decreased incidence of many cancers, improvement in fertility and a decrease in Polycystic Ovary Condition.

CHAPTER 4
CARBOHYDRATES

Many people are worried that they will have to give up carbohydrates on a low GI Diet. While this is the case for a lot of high protein diets, you can still enjoy these foods on the GI Diet if you choose the right type of carbohydrate.

Breads

A lot of breads have a very high GI because they are made from highly processed flour. This type of flour breaks down very quickly into glucose and has a fairly immediate impact on our blood sugar levels.

To work out the GI level of bread use the following guide:
- Look at the amount of fibre in the bread. The higher the fibre the better.

- Check the type of flour used. Rye flour, barley and wholemeal flour are all lower in GI.
- Choose whole grain bread. The coarser the grains the slower they are to be absorbed by the body and the slower the impact they have on your blood sugar levels.

So what types of bread should you eat while trying to eat low GI foods? Read the labels on supermarket breads and choose the ones that contain the most fibre and grains. Good choices include multigrain bread, rye bread, wholemeal sourdough bread, rye soy and linseed bread, soya bread and pumpernickel bread.

The breads to avoid include sliced white bread, bagels, French sticks or baguettes and white bread rolls.

Cereals

While many cereals are high GI there are a few low GI options. The important thing to remember with cereals is the shape and size of the grains and how processed they are. Cereals that are raw, with large grains have a much lower GI than those that are highly refined. This is why porridge, natural muesli and All-Bran are all good choices for sustained energy release.

Although some cereals high in sugar have a low or medium GI these are still best avoided. Examples of such cereals include Froot Loops and Nutri-Grain. High GI cereals to avoid are honey cereals, sugary cereals, flaked cereals, puffed rice and wheat cereals.

Potatoes

Potatoes are a great source of fibre, vitamin C and potassium but unfortunately most types of potato are high in GI. This is thought to be due to their high levels of starch.

Potato chips actually have a lower GI than boiled or steamed potatoes. This is because fat slows the rate at which food is emptied from the stomach. However this does not mean that potato chips are a better choice nutritionally. High levels of saturated fat are dangerous for coronary health.

New potatoes have the lowest GI levels of all types of potatoes and are the best choice. Sweet potatoes are high in fibre and have a lower GI than other varieties. Yams are also a good choice, but are not as readily available as new potatoes and sweet potatoes.

Rice

The basic determiner of the GI level in rice is the type of starch that it contains. Amylose (which is tightly boned together) has a lower GI because it breaks down more slowly than amylopectin (which has larger, more open molecules and therefore breaks down and is digested more quickly).

Jasmine rice, Calrose white rice and sticky rice all have a higher GI. The best rice to choose when you are trying to eat low GI foods is wild rice, brown rice and Basmati rice.

If you are in doubt about the GI level of rice a good rule of thumb is that the stickier the rice, the more likely it is to have a high GI.

Pasta

Pasta is actually much lower in GI than most people assume it to be. This is because most pasta is made from durum wheat flour, which is high in protein and also has fairly large starch particle due to the way the flour is ground.

If you eat your pasta 'al dente' rather then cooked until very soft you also help reduce its GI as the firmer pasta (like other less-cooked foods) is more slowly digested.

The only pasta that has a high GI is corn pasta, gluten-free pasta and tinned pasta.

Grains

Most grains are an excellent source of low GI energy and are full of nutrients. Grains have a low GI level because they are relatively unprocessed and they are also high in fibre.

Low GI choices include barley, buckwheat, bulgur (cracked wheat), quinoa and semolina. Higher GI levels are found in couscous and millet.

CHAPTER 5
FRUIT AND VEGETABLES

Fruit and vegetables are an essential part of any healthy balanced diet. They are generally fat-free, high in fibre, full of vitamins and minerals and low-carb.

Fruit

Because fruit is sweet and easily digested it is a surprise to find that most fruits are either low or medium in their GI levels. This is because the main sugar in fruit (fructose) has to be converted into glucose before it can be used as a source of energy. This conversion process slows down the rate at which it affects blood sugar levels.

Apart from fructose levels, the other factors that affect the GI levels of a fruit are its acidity (the higher the acidity, the lower its GI), its fibre content (the higher the fibre, the lower the GI) and how processed it is. Fruit juice has a higher GI than the same fruit in its raw form because the juice has less fibre. Canned fruits are more quickly digested by the body and therefore have a higher GI as well.

The highest GI fruits are fruit juices, dried fruits and canned fruits. Watermelon also has a high GI because it contains sucrose rather than fructose (which most fruits contain). Despite its high GI level, watermelon does not effect blood sugar levels as much as other high GI foods because it actually has very little carb, so it is still okay to eat.

Sweet soft fruits such as apricots, cherries, honeydew, pawpaw and rockmelon as well as most dried fruits have a medium GI. All other fruits are low GI and are an excellent source of sustained energy.

Vegetables

Although vegetables are classified as a carbohydrate, they actually contain only a small amount of carbohydrate. This means that most vegetables are low GI except for a few of the starchy root vegetables, such as parsnips, swedes and turnips.

Most types of potatoes have a very high GI, except for new potatoes. Potatoes cooked in fat (such as potato chips and French fries) also have a lower GI due to the effect of fat on the rate of absorption but they are not recommended due to the health problems linked to consumption of high levels of fat.

Canned beetroot comes in with a medium GI, but all other vegetables have a low GI. This is because they generally have high fibre levels. Canning and processing vegetables does slightly increase their GI levels but this effect is minimal and these foods are still an excellent source of vitamins, minerals and fibre.

CHAPTER 6
DRINKS

Water is by far your best choice of beverage, along with herbal teas or diet soft drinks if you want something sweet.

Spirits, beer and wine all have a low GI, but alcohol should always be consumed in moderation.

The worst beverages are sweetened fruit juices, sports drinks, prune juice, and caffeinated soft drinks.

CHAPTER 7
FATS AND PROTEINS

Fats help reduce the GI of many carbohydrates because they slow down the rate at which foods are absorbed by the stomach. Many high-fat foods are low GI but this does not mean that they can be eaten in large quantities. For a low GI diet to be healthy the right type of fats need to be included.

Healthy fats are the monounsaturated fats found in vegetables (olives, nuts, seeds, avocadoes, as well as the oils made from these) and the polyunsaturated fats that come from oily fish, such as trout and salmon.

There are many serious health risks associated with a diet high in saturated fats (such as butter, meat fat, full-fat dairy products) and trans fats (palm oil, margarine, commercial cakes and biscuits). The other problem with fats is that they are high in calories and this causes problems for people who are trying to lose weight. Proteins and low GI carbs are far more filling with a lower calorie count than the equivalent serve of a high-fat food.

Meats

Pure proteins have no carbs and so they have a GI of 0. When consuming proteins as part of a healthy diet try to avoid saturated fat. Good choices are lean beef, chicken, ham, lamb, pork, venison and veal.

The other thing to watch is the sodium content of some proteins. Anchovies, bacon, and processed meats all contain high levels of sodium and should be consumed in moderation.

Processed meats such as chicken nuggets and schnitzels have a slightly higher GI due to the addition of breadcrumbs and fillers. Even though their GI is only slightly higher than unprocessed meats pure protein foods are a better choice.

Seeds and nuts

These are an excellent source of protein and full of nutrients and energy. Seeds and nuts are an excellent snack food, providing sustained energy. The only thing to watch with nuts and seeds is their calorie density—try not to eat too many if you want to loose weight. Although they are packed with good fats, they are still high in calories.

Seafood

Fresh fish is an excellent, low GI choice. Clams, crab, fish, lobster, mussels, oysters, prawns, sardines, scallops, squid, tuna and salmon are all low GI. Avoid battered and deep-fried seafood as this raises both the GI and the fat levels. Sashimi is a better choice than sushi if you are eating Japanese because the rice in sushi has a high GI.

Smoked seafood products are still low in GI but can contain higher levels of sodium so they should be consumed in moderation.

CHAPTER 8
GI FOR THE FAMILY

For children, in particular, there are several benefits from the inclusion of low GI foods into the family's diet. These include:

Establishment of healthy eating habits
Low GI foods are generally higher in fibre and lower in sugar than their high GI counterparts. Low GI foods are also closer to their original state than high GI ones.

Elimination of preservatives and chemicals
Low GI foods are less processed and generally do not contain preservatives and additives.

Longer concentration and attention spans
Because low GI foods have a slow release of energy

they provide children with the sustained energy they need for learning and concentration as well as sport. This is why it is especially important that children eat a low GI breakfast before they go to school. A low GI lunch will help both adults and children avoid the after-lunch energy drop that many people experience, which leads to chocolate cravings and tiredness.

Reduced risk of developing obesity and diabetes

A low GI diet helps to control blood sugar levels (helping prevent diabetes) and dramatically reduces the consumption of highly processed foods that are loaded with sugar. Reducing the consumption of these foods helps reduce the risk of diabetes and obesity.

So there are many benefits that eating low GI foods within a balanced diet can bring to the whole family, not just for adults who want to lose weight.

CHAPTER 9
EASY WAYS TO LOWER YOUR GI

These simple rules will help you keep your blood sugar levels under control.

Try to eat something acidic with high GI foods

Because acid slows the rate at which food is absorbed the addition of acid can actually reduce a food's GI level. So a side salad with a vinaigrette dressing or a squeeze of lemon over vegetables or meats will help reduce the rate at which your blood sugar levels rise.

Eat low GI foods with high GI foods

Eating low GI foods at the same meal will reduce the effect of the high GI food on your blood sugar levels.

Eat at least 3 meals a day
Do not skip meals. If you have a long gap between meals your blood sugar levels will drop and you will crave high GI foods. Avoid these cravings by keeping a supply of low GI snacks with you at all times.

Eat smaller portions
If you want to indulge in a high GI food, just eat a smaller portion and accompany it with a low GI food. So instead of ordering a main meal, order an entrée size dish and accompany that with a large side salad.

CHAPTER 10
EATING OUT AND TAKE AWAY FOODS

Eating out is where people often have difficulty choosing healthy foods. With a few basic rules you can still go out and enjoy yourself while keeping in mind the principles of a low GI diet.

Have a low GI snack before you go
This will fill you up and give you sustained energy. If your only option when eating out is a high GI meal then have a small serve and accompany it with a side salad dressed with vinegar or lemon juice.

Fill up with water
Drink lots of water before you start drinking alcohol. This will help fill you up.

Substitute carbs with vegetables

Instead of filling up with carbs, ask for extra helpings of salads and vegetables. Say no to bread, potatoes, rice or cous cous and instead have a salad or extra steamed vegetables.

Ask for sauces and dressings to be served on the side

This is self evident but it can make a huge difference to the GI of your overall meal.

Below is a quick cuisine guide that will help you choose the healthiest option in restaurants and take away food.

The best choice column is foods which are low GI, and are a fresh and healthy choice. The worst choice column is foods which are high in GI and high in fat, sugar, sodium and calories.

CUISINE	★ BEST CHOICE – low GI	!!! WORST CHOICE – high GI
Italian	• Grilled meat or fish • Pasta with meat/seafood or tomato based sauce	• Risotto • Gnocchi • Garlic or herb bread • Pizza
Japanese	• Chicken teriyaki • Sashimi	• Sushi • Steamed rice
Indian	• Curries with meat, pulses or vegetables • Dahl • Wholemeal baked chappati • Low-fat yogurt	• Deep-fried entrees • Roti bread (or any other white fried bread) • Large serves of rice
Asian	• Steamed fish with ginger • Vegetarian and/or meat stir-fries with soy sauce	• Deep-fried entrees • Large serves of rice or noodles • Dumplings • Sweet stir-fries • Satay sauce
Greek	• Souvlaki • Greek salad	• Baklava • Dolmades • Moussaka
Seafood	• Steamed seafood • Salad	• Deep-fried seafood • Hot chips

CUISINE	★ BEST CHOICE – low GI	!!! WORST CHOICE – high GI
Modern Australian/ buffets	• Cold meats • Cold seafood • Salads • Fresh fruit	• Potato salad • Rice salad • Deep-fried food • Bread • Cakes • Cheesecakes • Mousse
Burger chains	• Diet soft drink • Salads plus menu	• Fries • Burgers • Nuggets
Sandwich shops	• Wholemeal sandwiches with meat and salad filling	• Schnitzel sandwiches • White bread sandwiches • Potato salad
Pizza Hut	• Diet soft drink • Salad bar (no potato or rice or creamy dressings)	• All pizzas • Garlic bread
Fish and chips	• Grilled fish • Green salad	• Fish (deep fried) • Potato chips • Potato scallops • Calamari

★ Low GI – good choice
!!! High GI – has immediate impact on blood sugar levels

CHAPTER 11
GI COUNTER – FOOD CATEGORIES

The GI counter has been divided into two chapters. The counter in this chapter is grouped by food categories in order to simplify use. This allows immediate comparison within food groups, allowing the reader to instantly see the low-GI alternative to any particular food. The counter in chapter 13 is an easy reference table in alphabetical order and provides the GI values for the most common foods.

Please remember that nutritional values vary greatly between specific brands so always read the label carefully before purchasing and consuming any product. For example, the GI levels of multigrain bread vary according to brand. Check the labels and purchase the one with the highest fibre content.

If there is a specific food that you cannot find on the counter then use the following principles when deciding between brands. The best option is usually the brand that contains the highest fibre, lower calories, lowest sugar and lowest fat (especially saturated fat). Remember when comparing products to compare the same serving size: recommended servings can very enormously between brands.

Both counters use the following headings:

★ Low GI (-50)
These foods are a good choice. They will have a steady impact on your blood sugar as their GI levels are 50 or under. They are the best choice within the particular food group and should form the basis of your diet.

! Low GI (-50)
These foods are a bad choice. They are low in GI but high in saturated fat, sodium, alcohol, caffeine or sugar and therefore consumption of them should be limited.

!! Medium GI (50-70)
These foods generally have a GI level of 50-70.

!!! High GI (70+)
These foods generally have a GI level of 70 plus and will have a fairly immediate impact on your blood sugar levels.

Beans and Legumes

★ LOW GI (-50)	! LOW GI (-50)	!! MEDIUM GI (50-70)	!!! HIGH GI (70+)
• Alfalfa sprouts • Baked beans • Black beans • Borlotti beans • Butter beans • Canned beans • Chickpeas • Dried beans • Green beans • Haricot beans			• Broad beans • Refried beans

★	**Low GI** – good choice
!	**Low GI** – bad choice: High in saturated fat, sodium or sugar
!!	**Medium GI** – eat in moderation
!!!	**High GI** – has immediate impact on blood sugar levels

★ LOW GI (-50)	! LOW GI (-50)	!! MEDIUM GI (50-70)	!!! HIGH GI (70+)
• Kidney beans • Lentils • Lima beans • Mung beans • Navy beans • Snake beans • Soya beans • Split peas			

Beverages

★ LOW GI (-50)	! LOW GI (-50)	!! MEDIUM GI (50-70)	!!! HIGH GI (70+)
• Bottled water • Diet soft drinks • Soda water • Tap water • Tea, herbal, no milk or sugar • Tomato juice • Tonic water	• Beer • Coffee, no milk or sugar • Spirits • Tea, black • Wine	• Apple juice, unsweetened • Fruit juice, unsweetened • Orange juice, unsweetened • Soft drinks	• Apple juice, sweetened • Caffeinated soft drinks (Pepsi, Coke, etc) • Fruit juice, sweetened • Lucozade • Orange juice,

★ LOW GI (-50)	! LOW GI (-50)	!! MEDIUM GI (50-70)	!!! HIGH GI (70+)
			sweetened • Prune juice, sweetened or unsweetened • Sports drinks (most brands) • Watermelon juice

Biscuits

Biscuits are best avoided or only eaten as an occasional treat due to their high levels of fat and sugar

★ LOW GI (-50)	! LOW GI (-50)	!! MEDIUM GI (50-70)	!!! HIGH GI (70+)
	• Oatmeal biscuits • Rich Tea biscuits	• Digestives • Milk arrowroot • Oatcakes • Shortbread • Shredded wheatmeal • Chocolate biscuits (plain)	• Cream filled wafer biscuits • Cream filled chocolate biscuits

Breads

★ LOW GI (-50)	! LOW GI (-50)	!! MEDIUM GI (50-70)	!!! HIGH GI (70+)
• Multigrain bread • Pumpernickel bread • Rye bread • Rye soy and linseed • Soy and linseed • Wholemeal sourdough bread • Soya bread		• Fruit bread • Pita bread • Tortillas • White sourdough	• Bagels • Baguettes • Bread crumbs • Bread stuffing • Croissants • Doughnuts • Hot dog buns • Melba toast • Sliced white bread • White bread rolls

Breakfast Cereals

★ LOW GI (-50)	! LOW GI (-50)	!! MEDIUM GI (50-70)	!!! HIGH GI (70+)
• All-Bran • Natural muesli (not toasted)	• Frosties	• Froot Loops • Just Right • Nutri-Grain	• Bran Flakes • Coco Pops • Corn Flakes

★	**Low GI** – good choice
!	**Low GI** – bad choice: High in saturated fat, sodium or sugar
!!	**Medium GI** – eat in moderation
!!!	**High GI** – has immediate impact on blood sugar levels

★ LOW GI (-50)	! LOW GI (-50)	!! MEDIUM GI (50-70)	!!! HIGH GI (70+)
• Oat bran • Porridge oats (traditional)		• Shredded wheat bran products (such as Mini-Wheats) • Special K • Vita-Brits • Weet-Bix	• Crispix • Golden Wheats • Porridge, instant • Rice Bubbles • Sultana Bran

Cakes and Pastries

Cakes are best avoided or only eaten as an occasional treat due to their high levels of fat and sugar

★ LOW GI (-50)	! LOW GI (-50)	!! MEDIUM GI (50-70)	!!! HIGH GI (70+)
	• Banana cake, homemade • Chocolate cake, packet, iced • Pound cake, plain • Sponge cake, un-iced and no cream	• Angel food cake • Croissants • Crumpets	• Cupcakes, iced • Lamingtons • Pikelets • Scones

Cereal, Grains, Rice

★ LOW GI (-50)	! LOW GI (-50)	!! MEDIUM GI (50-70)	!!! HIGH GI (70+)
• Barley • Buckwheat • Cracked wheat (bulgur) • Linseed • Quinoa • Semolina		• Arborio rice • Basmati rice • Brown rice • Long grain rice	• Calrose brown rice • Calrose white rice • Couscous • Jasmine rice • Millet • Short grain rice

Condiments, Herbs, Seasonings

★ LOW GI (-50)	! LOW GI (-50)	!! MEDIUM GI (50-70)	!!! HIGH GI (70+)
• Chilli (fresh, powdered, flakes) • Garlic • Herbs • Hommus	• Salt • Soy sauce		• Aioli Mayonnaise, whole egg • Tartare sauce • Tomato sauce

★	Low GI – good choice
!	Low GI – bad choice: High in saturated fat, sodium or sugar
!!	Medium GI – eat in moderation
!!!	High GI – has immediate impact on blood sugar levels

★ LOW GI (-50)	! LOW GI (-50)	!! MEDIUM GI (50-70)	!!! HIGH GI (70+)
• Lemon juice • Lime juice • Mayonnaise (fat free) • Mustard • Pepper • Soy sauce (reduced salt) • Spices • Tamari • Tzatziki • Teriyaki sauce • Worcestershire sauce			

Dairy

★ LOW GI (-50)	! LOW GI (-50)	!! MEDIUM GI (50-70)	!!! HIGH GI (70+)
• Cheese, reduced fat • Gelato, sugar free	• Butter • Cheese, full fat • Custard,	• Condensed milk	• Rice milk

★ LOW GI (-50)	! LOW GI (-50)	!! MEDIUM GI (50-70)	!!! HIGH GI (70+)
• Ice-cream, reduced fat • Milk, reduced fat • Milk, skim • Yogurt	homemade • Eggs • Gelato • Ice-cream, full fat • Milk, full fat		

Fats, Oils, Nuts

★ LOW GI (-50)	! LOW GI (-50)	!! MEDIUM GI (50-70)	!!! HIGH GI (70+)
• Nuts, unsalted • Olive oil • Polyunsaturated fats • Pumpkin seeds • Sesame seeds • Sunflower seeds	• Butter • Dairy fat • Meat fat • Nuts, salted • Trans fats		

★	**Low GI** – good choice
!	**Low GI** – bad choice: High in saturated fat, sodium or sugar
!!	**Medium GI** – eat in moderation
!!!	**High GI** – has immediate impact on blood sugar levels

Fruit

★ LOW GI (-50)	! LOW GI (-50)	!! MEDIUM GI (50-70)	!!! HIGH GI (70+)
• Apples • Apple sauce • Avocadoes • Bananas • Blackberries • Blueberries • Figs • Grapefruit • Grapes • Kiwifruit • Lemons • Limes • Mandarins • Mango • Nectarines • Oranges • Peaches		• Apricots, fresh and dried • Cherries • Cranberries, dried • Dried fruits • Honeydew • Pawpaw • Pineapple • Raisins • Rockmelon • Sultanas	• Dates • Lychees, canned in syrup • Watermelon

★ **Low GI** – good choice
! **Low GI** – bad choice: High in saturated fat, sodium or sugar
!! **Medium GI** – eat in moderation
!!! **High GI** – has immediate impact on blood sugar levels

★ LOW GI (-50)	! LOW GI (-50)	!! MEDIUM GI (50-70)	!!! HIGH GI (70+)
• Pears • Plums • Prunes • Raspberries • Rhubarb • Strawberries • Canned fruit			

Meat and Poultry

★ LOW GI (-50)	! LOW GI (-50)	!! MEDIUM GI (50-70)	!!! HIGH GI (70+)
• Beef, lean • Chicken, lean • Duck, lean • Ham • Lamb • Pork, lean • Veal • Venison	• Anchovies • Bacon • Beef with fat on • Carpaccio • Chicken with skin on • Chicken nuggets • Duck with skin on • Eggs • Mince, high fat		

★ LOW GI (-50)	! LOW GI (-50)	!! MEDIUM GI (50-70)	!!! HIGH GI (70+)
	• Processed meats (sausages, hot dogs, etc) • Salami		

Noodles

★ LOW GI (-50)	! LOW GI (-50)	!! MEDIUM GI (50-70)	!!! HIGH GI (70+)
• Fresh rice noodles • Glass noodles • Mung bean (cellophane) noodles • Soba noodles	• 2 minute noodles	• Udon rice noodles	• Egg noodles • Hokkien noodles • Wheat noodles fresh) • Wheat noodles (dried)

Pasta

★ LOW GI (-50)	! LOW GI (-50)	!! MEDIUM GI (50-70)	!!! HIGH GI (70+)
• Capellini • Fettuccine • Linguine • Macaroni • Penne • Ravioli • Rigatoni • Shell pasta • Spaghetti • Vermicelli • Wholemeal durum wheat pasta • White durum wheat pasta	• Lasagna	• Macaroni and cheese	• Corn pasta • Gluten free pastas • Canned pastas • Rice pasta

★	Low GI – good choice
!	Low GI – bad choice: High in saturated fat, sodium or sugar
!!	Medium GI – eat in moderation
!!!	High GI – has immediate impact on blood sugar levels

Seafood

★ LOW GI (-50)	! LOW GI (-50)	!! MEDIUM GI (50-70)	!!! HIGH GI (70+)
• Clams • Crab • Fish, all types • Lobster • Mussels • Oysters • Prawns • Sardines • Sashimi • Scallops • Squid • Tuna and salmon, fresh or canned, in oil or brine	• Anchovies • Smoked oyster • Smoked mussels • Smoked salmon • Smoked trout		

★	**Low GI**	– good choice
!	**Low GI**	– bad choice: High in saturated fat, sodium or sugar
!!	**Medium GI**	– eat in moderation
!!!	**High GI**	– has immediate impact on blood sugar levels

Snack Foods

★ LOW GI (-50)	! LOW GI (-50)	!! MEDIUM GI (50-70)	!!! HIGH GI (70+)
• Fresh, canned fruits • Nuts, unsalted and raw • Pumpkin seeds • Sunflower seeds • Most chocolate bars • Potato chips	• Chocolate, milk • Corn chips	• Fruit fingers • Marshmallows • Mars Bars • Muesli bar, crunchy with dried fruit	• Burger Rings • Doughnuts • French Fries • Jelly Beans • Liquorice • Popcorn • Pretzels • Roll-Ups • Skittles • Twisties • Waffles

Soups

★ LOW GI (-50)	! LOW GI (-50)	!! MEDIUM GI (50-70)	!!! HIGH GI (70+)
• Consommé • Homemade vegetable or chicken soup	• Tomato soup, canned • Chicken noodle soup, commercial	• Split pea, canned	• Canned creamy soups

Spreads, Sugars and Sweeteners

★ LOW GI (-50)	! LOW GI (-50)	!! MEDIUM GI (50-70)	!!! HIGH GI (70+)
• Hommus • Peanut butter, reduced salt • Tahini	• Maple syrup, pure • Nutella • Peanut butter	• Golden syrup • Honey • Jam, strawberry	

Vegetables

★ LOW GI (-50)	! LOW GI (-50)	!! MEDIUM GI (50-70)	!!! HIGH GI (70+)
• Alfalfa • Artichokes • Asparagus • Bean sprouts • Broccoli • Canned vegetables • Corn • Carrots • Cabbage • Cauliflower • Celery		• Beetroot, canned	• Parsnips • Pumpkin • Sweet potatoes • Swedes • Turnips

★ LOW GI (-50)	! LOW GI (-50)	!! MEDIUM GI (50-70)	!!! HIGH GI (70+)
• Cucumber • Eggplant • Fennel • Green beans • Leeks • Lettuce • Mushrooms • Onion			

★	**Low GI** – good choice
!	**Low GI** – bad choice: High in saturated fat, sodium or sugar
!!	**Medium GI** – eat in moderation
!!!	**High GI** – has immediate impact on blood sugar levels

CHAPTER 12
GI COUNTER

This GI counter is an easy reference table in alphabetical order and provides the GI values for the most common foods.

	★ LOW GI (-50)	! LOW GI (-50)	!! MEDIUM GI (50-70)	!!! HIGH GI (70+)
2 minute noodles		!		
Aioli				!!!
Alfalfa sprouts	★			
All-Bran	★			
Anchovies		!		
Angel food cake			!!	
Apple juice, sweetened				!!!
Apple juice, unsweetened			!!	
Apple sauce	★			
Apples	★			
Apricots, fresh and dried			!!	

	★ LOW GI (-50)	! LOW GI (-50)	!! MEDIUM GI (50-70)	!!! HIGH GI (70+)
Arborio rice			!!	
Artichokes	★			
Asparagus	★			
Avocadoes	★			
Bacon		!		
Bagels				!!!
Baguettes				!!!
Baked beans	★			
Banana cake, homemade		!		
Bananas	★			
Barley	★			
Basmati rice			!!	
Bean sprouts	★			
Beans, baked	★			
Beans, black	★			
Beans, Borlotti	★			
Beans, broad				!!!
Beans, butter	★			
Beans, canned	★			
Beans, dried	★			
Beans, green	★			

★ **Low GI** – good choice
! **Low GI** – bad choice: High in saturated fat, sodium or sugar
!! **Medium GI** – eat in moderation
!!! **High GI** – has immediate impact on blood sugar levels

	★ LOW GI (-50)	! LOW GI (-50)	!! MEDIUM GI (50-70)	!!! HIGH GI (70+)
Beans, haricot	★			
Beans, kidney	★			
Beans, lima	★			
Beans, mung	★			
Beans, navy	★			
Beans, refried				!!!
Beans, snake	★			
Beans, soya	★			
Beef with fat on		!		
Beef, lean	★			
Beer		!		
Beetroot, canned			!!	
Biscuits, chocolate (plain)			!!	
Biscuits, cream filled chocolate				!!!
Biscuits, cream filled wafer				!!!
Biscuits, oatmeal		!		
Biscuits, Rich Tea		!		
Black beans	★			
Black tea		!		
Blackberries	★			
Blueberries	★			
Borlotti beans	★			
Bottled water	★			
Bran Flakes				!!!
Bread, fruit			!!	

	★ LOW GI (-50)	! LOW GI (-50)	!! MEDIUM GI (50-70)	!!! HIGH GI (70+)
Bread, multigrain	★			
Bread, pita			!!	
Bread, pumpernickel	★			
Bread, rye	★			
Bread, rye soy and linseed	★			
Bread, sliced white				!!!
Bread, soy and linseed	★			
Bread, soya	★			
Bread, white sourdough			!!	
Bread, wholemeal sourdough	★			
Bread crumbs				!!!
Bread rolls, white				!!!
Bread stuffing				!!!
Broad beans			!!	
Broccoli	★			
Brown rice			!!	
Brown rice, Calrose				!!!
Buckwheat	★			
Bulgur, cracked wheat	★			
Buns, hot dog				!!!
Burger Rings				!!!

★ **Low GI** – good choice
! **Low GI** – bad choice: High in saturated fat, sodium or sugar
!! **Medium GI** – eat in moderation
!!! **High GI** – has immediate impact on blood sugar levels

	★ LOW GI (-50)	! LOW GI (-50)	!! MEDIUM GI (50-70)	!!! HIGH GI (70+)
Butter		!		
Butter beans	★			
Cabbage	★			
Caffeinated soft drinks (Pepsi, Coke, etc)				!!!
Cake, angel food			!!	
Cake, banana (homemade)		!		
Cake, chocolate, iced (packet)		!		
Cake, sponge, un-iced and no cream		!		
Calrose brown rice				!!!
Calrose white rice				!!!
Canned beans	★			
Canned beetroot			!!	
Canned creamy soups				!!!
Canned fruit	★			
Canned lychees in syrup				!!!
Canned pastas				!!!
Canned split pea soup			!!	
Canned tomato soup		!		
Canned tuna and salmon, in oil or brine	★			
Canned vegetables	★			
Capellini	★			
Capsicum	★			
Carpaccio		!		

	★ LOW GI (-50)	! LOW GI (-50)	!! MEDIUM GI (50-70)	!!! HIGH GI (70+)
Carrots	★			
Cauliflower	★			
Celery	★			
Cheese, full fat		!		
Cheese, reduced fat	★			
Cherries			!!	
Chickpeas	★			
Chicken, lean	★			
Chicken noodle soup, commercial			!!	
Chicken nuggets		!		
Chicken noodle soup, commercial			!!	
Chicken with skin on		!		
Chilli (fresh, powdered, flakes)	★			
Chips, corn		!		
Chips, potato		!		
Chocolate bars		!		
Chocolate biscuits (plain)			!!	
Chocolate cake packet, iced		!		
Chocolate, milk		!		
Clams	★			
Coco Pops				!!!

★ **Low GI** – good choice
! **Low GI** – bad choice: High in saturated fat, sodium or sugar
!! **Medium GI** – eat in moderation
!!! **High GI** – has immediate impact on blood sugar levels

	★ LOW GI (-50)	! LOW GI (-50)	!! MEDIUM GI (50-70)	!!! HIGH GI (70+)
Coffee, no milk or sugar		!		
Condensed milk			!!	
Consommé	★			
Corn chips, plain		!		
Corn Flakes				!!!
Corn on the cob	★			
Corn pasta				!!!
Couscous				!!!
Crab	★			
Cracked wheat (bulgur)	★			
Cranberries, dried			!!	
Cream filled chocolate biscuits				!!!
Cream filled wafer biscuits				!!!
Crispix				!!!
Croissants			!!	
Crumpets			!!	
Cucumber	★			
Cupcakes, iced				!!!
Custard, homemade		!		
Dairy fat		!		
Dates				!!!
Diet soft drinks	★			
Digestives			!!	
Doughnuts				!!!
Dried apricots			!!	

	★ LOW GI (-50)	! LOW GI (-50)	!! MEDIUM GI (50-70)	!!! HIGH GI (70+)
Dried beans	★			
Dried cranberries			!!	
Dried fruits			!!	
Duck, lean	★			
Duck with skin on		!		
Durum wheat pasta, white	★			
Durum wheat pasta, wholemeal	★			
Egg noodles				!!!
Eggplant	★			
Eggs		!		
Fat, dairy		!		
Fat free mayonnaise	★			
Fat, meat		!		
Fats, polyunsaturated	★			
Fats, trans		!		
Fennel	★			
Fettuccine	★			
Figs	★			
Fish, all types	★			
French fries				!!!
Fresh and dried apricots			!!	

★	**Low GI** – good choice
!	**Low GI** – bad choice: High in saturated fat, sodium or sugar
!!	**Medium GI** – eat in moderation
!!!	**High GI** – has immediate impact on blood sugar levels

	★ LOW GI (-50)	! LOW GI (-50)	!! MEDIUM GI (50-70)	!!! HIGH GI (70+)
Fresh rice noodles	★			
Fresh, canned or dried fruits	★			
Fresh tuna and salmon, in oil or brine	★			
Froot Loops			!!	
Frosties		!		
Fruit bread			!!	
Fruit, canned	★			
Fruit fingers			!!	
Fruit juice, sweetened				!!!
Fruit juice, unsweetened			!!	
Fruits, dried			!!	
Full fat cheese		!		
Full fat ice-cream		!		
Full fat milk		!		
Garlic	★			
Gelato		!		
Gelato, sugar free	★			
Glass noodles	★			
Gluten free pastas				!!!
Golden syrup			!!	
Golden Wheats				!!!
Grapefruit	★			
Grapes	★			
Green beans	★			
Ham	★			

	★ LOW GI (-50)	! LOW GI (-50)	!! MEDIUM GI (50-70)	!!! HIGH GI (70+)
Haricot beans	★			
Herbal tea, no milk or sugar	★			
Herbs	★			
High fat mince		!		
Hokkien noodles				!!!
Homemade banana cake		!		
Homemade custard		!		
Homemade vegetable or chicken soup	★			
Hommus	★			
Honey			!!	
Honeydew			!!	
Hot dog buns				!!!
Ice-cream, full fat		!		
Ice-cream, reduced fat	★			
Iced chocolate cake, packet		!		
Iced cupcakes				!!!
Jam			!!	
Jasmine rice				!!!
Jelly beans				!!!
Juice, apple, sweetened				!!!

★ **Low GI** – good choice
! **Low GI** – bad choice: High in saturated fat, sodium or sugar
!! **Medium GI** – eat in moderation
!!! **High GI** – has immediate impact on blood sugar levels

	★ LOW GI (-50)	! LOW GI (-50)	!! MEDIUM GI (50-70)	!!! HIGH GI (70+)
Juice, apple, unsweetened			!!	
Juice, fruit, sweetened				!!!
Juice, fruit, unsweetened			!!	
Juice, orange, sweetened				!!!
Juice, lemon	★			
Juice, lime	★			
Juice, orange, unsweetened			!!	
Juice, prune				!!!
Juice, tomato	★			
Juice, watermelon				!!!
Just Right			!!	
Kidney beans	★			
Kiwifruit	★			
Lamb	★			
Lamingtons				!!!
Lasagna		!		
Lean beef	★			
Lean chicken	★			
Lean duck	★			
Lean pork	★			
Leeks	★			
Lemon juice	★			
Lemons	★			
Lentils	★			
Lettuce	★			

	★ LOW GI (-50)	! LOW GI (-50)	!! MEDIUM GI (50-70)	!!! HIGH GI (70+)
Lima beans	★			
Lime juice	★			
Limes	★			
Linguine	★			
Linseed	★			
Liquorice				!!!
Lobster	★			
Long grain rice			!!	
Lucozade				!!!
Lychees, canned in syrup				!!!
Macaroni	★			
Macaroni and cheese			!!	
Mandarins	★			
Mango	★			
Maple syrup, pure		!		
Mars Bars			!!	
Marshmallows			!!	
Mayonnaise, fat free	★			
Mayonnaise, whole egg				!!!
Meat fat		!		
Meats, processed		!		

★	**Low GI** – good choice
!	**Low GI** – bad choice: High in saturated fat, sodium or sugar
!!	**Medium GI** – eat in moderation
!!!	**High GI** – has immediate impact on blood sugar levels

	★ LOW GI (-50)	! LOW GI (-50)	!! MEDIUM GI (50-70)	!!! HIGH GI (70+)
Melba toast				!!!
Milk arrowroot			!!	
Milk chocolate		!		
Milk, condensed			!!	
Milk, full fat		!		
Milk, reduced fat	★			
Milk, rice				!!!
Milk, skim	★			
Millet				!!!
Mince, high fat		!		
Mini-Wheats			!!	
Monosaturated fats (found in vegetables or made from vegetables)	★			
Most chocolate bars		!		
Muesli, natural (not toasted)	★			
Muesli bar, crunchy with dried fruit			!!	
Multigrain bread	★			
Mung bean noodles (cellophane)	★			
Mung beans	★			
Mushrooms	★			
Mussels	★			
Mussels, smoked		!		
Mustard	★			
Natural muesli (not toasted)	★			

	★ LOW GI (-50)	! LOW GI (-50)	!! MEDIUM GI (50-70)	!!! HIGH GI (70+)
Navy beans	★			
Nectarines	★			
Noodles, cellophane	★			
Noodles, egg				!!!
Noodles, fresh rice	★			
Noodles, glass	★			
Noodles, hokkien				!!!
Noodles, mung bean	★			
Noodles, rice, fresh	★			
Noodles, rice, udon			!!	
Noodles, soba	★			
Noodles, 2 minute		!		
Noodles, udon rice			!!	
Noodles, wheat (dried)				!!!
Noodles, wheat (fresh)				!!!
Nutella		!		
Nutri-Grain			!!	
Nuts, salted		!		
Nuts, unsalted	★			
Nuts, unsalted and raw	★			
Oat bran	★			

★	**Low GI** – good choice
!	**Low GI** – bad choice: High in saturated fat, sodium or sugar
!!	**Medium GI** – eat in moderation
!!!	**High GI** – has immediate impact on blood sugar levels

	★ LOW GI (-50)	! LOW GI (-50)	!! MEDIUM GI (50-70)	!!! HIGH GI (70+)
Oatcakes			!!	
Oatmeal biscuits		!		
Oats, porridge (traditional)	★			
Oil, olive	★			
Onions	★			
Orange juice, sweetened				!!!
Orange juice, unsweetened			!!	
Oranges	★			
Oyster, smoked		!		
Oysters	★			
Parsnips				!!!
Pasta, corn				!!!
Pasta, rice				!!!
Pasta, shell	★			
Pasta, white durum wheat	★			
Pasta, wholemeal durum wheat	★			
Pastas, canned				!!!
Pastas, gluten free				!!!
Pawpaw			!!	
Peaches	★			
Peanut butter		!		
Peanut butter, reduced salt	★			
Pears	★			
Peas	★			
Peas, split	★			

	★ LOW GI (-50)	! LOW GI (-50)	!! MEDIUM GI (50-70)	!!! HIGH GI (70+)
Penne	★			
Pepper	★			
Pikelets				!!!
Pineapple			!!	
Pita bread			!!	
Plums	★			
Polyunsaturated fats (found in fish)	★			
Popcorn				!!!
Pork, lean	★			
Porridge, instant				!!!
Porridge oats (traditional)	★			
Potato chips		!		
Potatoes, all other types				!!!
Potatoes, new			!!	
Potatoes, sweet				!!!
Pound cake, plain		!		
Prawns	★			
Pretzels				
Processed meats (sausages, hot dogs, etc)				!!!
Prune juice				!!!

★   **Low GI** – good choice
!   **Low GI** – bad choice: High in saturated fat, sodium or sugar
!! **Medium GI** – eat in moderation
!!! **High GI** – has immediate impact on blood sugar levels

	★ LOW GI (-50)	! LOW GI (-50)	!! MEDIUM GI (50-70)	!!! HIGH GI (70+)
Prunes	★			
Pumpernickel bread	★			
Pumpkin				!!!
Pumpkin seeds	★			
Quinoa	★			
Radish	★			
Raisins			!!	
Raspberries	★			
Ravioli	★			
Reduced fat ice-cream	★			
Reduced fat milk	★			
Reduced salt peanut butter	★			
Refried beans			!!	
Rhubarb	★			
Rice, arborio			!!	
Rice, basmati			!!	
Rice, brown			!!	
Rice, Calrose brown				!!!
Rice, Calrose white				!!!
Rice, jasmine				!!!
Rice, long grain			!!	
Rice, short grain				!!!
Rice Bubbles				!!!
Rice milk				!!!
Rice noodles, fresh	★			

	★ LOW GI (-50)	! LOW GI (-50)	!! MEDIUM GI (50-70)	!!! HIGH GI (70+)
Rice noodles, udon				!!!
Rice pasta				!!!
Rich Tea biscuits		!		
Rigatoni	★			
Rocket	★			
Rockmelon			!!	
Roll-Ups				!!!
Rye bread	★			
Rye, soy and linseed bread	★			
Salami		!		
Salmon and tuna, fresh or canned, in oil or brine	★			
Salmon, smoked		!		
Salt		!		
Salted nuts		!		
Sardines	★			
Sashimi	★			
Sauce, apple	★			
Sauce, soy		!		
Sauce, soy (reduced salt)	★			
Sauce, tartare				!!!

★	**Low GI** – good choice
!	**Low GI** – bad choice: High in saturated fat, sodium or sugar
!!	**Medium GI** – eat in moderation
!!!	**High GI** – has immediate impact on blood sugar levels

	★ LOW GI (-50)	! LOW GI (-50)	!! MEDIUM GI (50-70)	!!! HIGH GI (70+)
Sauce, tomato				!!!
Scallops	★			
Scones				!!!
Seeds, pumpkin	★			
Seeds, sesame	★			
Seeds, sunflower	★			
Semolina	★			
Sesame seeds	★			
Shell pasta	★			
Short grain rice				!!!
Shortbread			!!	
Shredded wheat bran products (such as Mini-Wheats)			!!	
Shredded wheatmeal			!!	
Skim milk	★			
Skittles				!!!
Sliced white bread				!!!
Smoked mussels		!		
Smoked oyster		!		
Smoked salmon		!		
Smoked trout		!		
Snake beans	★			
Soba noodles	★			
Soda water	★			
Soft drinks			!!	

	★ LOW GI (-50)	! LOW GI (-50)	!! MEDIUM GI (50-70)	!!! HIGH GI (70+)
Soft drinks, caffeinated (Pepsi, Coke, etc)			!!	
Soft drinks, diet	★			
Soups, canned creamy				!!!
Soup, chicken noodle commercial			!!	
Soup, homemade vegetable or chicken	★			
Soup, split pea, canned			!!	
Soup, tomato, canned		!		
Soy and linseed bread	★			
Soy sauce		!		
Soy sauce (reduced salt)	★			
Soya beans				
Soya bread	★			
Spaghetti	★			
Special K			!!	
Spices	★			
Spinach	★			
Spirits		!		
Split pea, canned			!!	
Split peas	★			

★	**Low GI** – good choice
!	**Low GI** – bad choice: High in saturated fat, sodium or sugar
!!	**Medium GI** – eat in moderation
!!!	**High GI** – has immediate impact on blood sugar levels

	★ LOW GI (-50)	! LOW GI (-50)	!! MEDIUM GI (50-70)	!!! HIGH GI (70+)
Sponge cake, un-iced and no cream	★			
Sports drinks (most brands)				!!!
Sprouts, alfalfa	★			
Sprouts, bean	★			
Squid	★			
Strawberries	★			
Strawberry jam			!!	
Sultana Bran				!!!
Sultanas			!!	
Sunflower seeds	★			
Sushi				!!!
Swedes				!!!
Sweet potatoes				!!!
Syrup, canned lychees in				!!!
Syrup, golden			!!	
Syrup, maple, pure		!		
Tahini	★			
Tamari	★			
Tap water	★			
Tartare sauce				!!!
Tea, black		!		
Tea, herbal, no milk or sugar	★			
Teriyaki sauce	★			
Tinned fruit	★			
Tinned pastas				!!!

	★ LOW GI (-50)	! LOW GI (-50)	!! MEDIUM GI (50-70)	!!! HIGH GI (70+)
Toast, Melba				!!!
Tomato juice	★			
Tomato sauce				!!!
Tomato soup, canned			!!	
Tonic water	★			
Tortillas			!!	
Trans fats (found in processed foods such as biscuits, margarines and cakes)		!		
Trout, smoked		!		
Tuna and salmon, fresh or canned, in oil or brine	★			
Turnips				!!!
Twisties				!!!
Udon rice noodles			!!	
Unsalted and raw nuts	★			
Unsalted nuts	★			
Veal	★			
Vegetables, canned	★			
Venison	★			
Vermicelli	★			

★	**Low GI** – good choice
!	**Low GI** – bad choice: High in saturated fat, sodium or sugar
!!	**Medium GI** – eat in moderation
!!!	**High GI** – has immediate impact on blood sugar levels

	★ LOW GI (-50)	! LOW GI (-50)	!! MEDIUM GI (50-70)	!!! HIGH GI (70+)
Vita-Brits			!!	
Waffles				!!!
Water, bottled	★			
Water, soda	★			
Water, tap	★			
Water, tonic	★			
Watermelon				!!!
Watermelon juice				!!!
Weet-Bix			!!	
Wheat, cracked, bulgur	★			
Wheat noodles, dried				!!!
Wheat noodles, fresh				!!!
Wheat pasta, durum, white	★			
Wheat pasta, durum, wholemeal	★			
Wheatmeal biscuits, shredded			!!	
White bread, sliced				!!!
White bread rolls				!!!
White rice, Calrose				!!!
White sourdough bread			!!	
Wholemeal sourdough bread	★			
Wine		!		
Worcestershire sauce	★			
Yogurt	★			
Zucchini	★			